My Spoken Word Wife:

Playing for Keeps

I0623897

Misael Juarez

Also available by Barrio Blues Press

Nation: A Poetry Book by Penned in the City
(October 2020)

Unity, Volume 1: A Magical Realism Anthology
(December 2020)

Wolf Trek: A Post-Apocalyptic Werewolf Novelette
(January 2021)

My Spoken Word Wife:

Playing for Keeps

Misael Juarez

Edited by
Daniel Brooks and
María J. Estrada

BARRIO BLUES PRESS
Chicago 2022

FIRST BARRIO BLUES PRESS EDITION, JUNE 2022
My Spoken Word Wife
Copyright © 2022 by Misael Juarez
Book design by María J. Estrada
Cover design © PritiJ of PritiJ Designs and Andjela Vujić
Cover art © Halo
Internal art © pngtree.com

Published by Barrio Blues Press
Chicago, IL 60609
Barriobluespress.com
(312) 685-1602
Barrio Blues Press Trade Paperback: ISBN: 978-1-954444-01-0
eBook: ISBN: 9781954444003

Printed in the United States of America

This book is dedicated to all those people, fighting for a better world.

Contents

Foreword

Steve Teixeira

When Misael Juarez's teacher told me, "His writing is powerful—and yet he can't write," I knew she didn't mean it as an insult. She was trying to explain how his writing could be so effective, even though he didn't seem to know many of the rules of so-called proper writing.

When she encountered that dynamic collision between Misael's writing and writing rules, she had bumped into the contradictory essence of who he is: a thoughtful man who has lived a reckless youth; a gentle spirit who sometimes became aggressive; a source of creative energy despite a self-destructive past.

Misael Juarez is a writer and a poet because that is what he does, not because he was ever professionally approved to do it. Nowhere does his academic record at Cal State L.A., where I first met him, proclaim that he is a writer. Neither does his bank account.

He did not start to write, and constantly keeps doing it, to earn the approval of those kinds of institutions. He told me he did it because *writing was his way to survive the hostile social system that confronts him*. I would add that his poetry is his way of helping others to survive, not by hiding from oppressors, but by exposing them. Excerpts from his work make this stance clear:

"The Word Doctor's Medicine" (excerpt)
Making money is a curse if you're full of greed

Don't respect billionaires when kids sleep on concrete

The crowd roars at my shows when I let them all know
Fighting injustice provides you with a bold soul

"Bombs and Poets" (excerpt)
Women take the lit stage and spit their grievances
Rhyming precisely for the exploited seamstress
It don't take a college degree to make demands
When you make the crowd roar with a microphone stand

"The Jaguar 45" (excerpt)
My time in jail taught me it's a marketing scheme
Appealing to scare folks that punishment heals fiends
Kids are sent from schools to the prison industry
That's legal human trafficking if you ask me

And yet, *My Spoken Word Wife* is also a book of
hope, because after surviving a world that could have killed
him, or broken his spirit, he sees us and stands side-by-side
with us:

"Made for Rap" (excerpt)
I see those hard-working people without the fear
Making this country great with their blood, sweat, and
tears

It's expensive to support the habits of the rich
They hoard wealth while ignoring the impoverished

Returning back home after being stranded at sea
Rocking metaphors like they are my golden fleece

"Graffiti Angels 1996" (excerpt)
All the homies searched for visible spots to graff
As cops surveilled like End of Watch while we all laughed

Gentrification brought rich folks with .44s
Landowners who turned old buildings into condos

Raising the rent on the poor like they are heartless
Developers kicked families out apartments
New residents scored drugs in their brand-new Jaguars
Crying the city is full of graffiti wars

And taggers from L.A. were some of the baddest
We were rebels with no money for a canvas

But Misael has a broader, deeper vision than just
what's painted on a wall. This "L.A. Zapotec," as he calls
himself, reads and learns as well as writes. From the streets
of Oaxaca, México to the Harvard Street barrio in Los
Angeles, he refers to perils but also possibilities for a better
future. He says his *Spoken Word Wife* inspired him to see
this truth—and she will inspire readers.

"Revolutionary Dreams" (excerpt)
So, I never look back or down on my bad luck
It's never late to write a flight for sitting ducks
But if the economy wishes automation
Then, we're mighty ducks to ask for revolution

Editor's Notes

María J. Estrada

When I founded Barrio Blues Press in the summer of 2020, my aim was to elevate the voices of emerging writers, especially those that envisioned a cooperative society. I wanted a press that countered the narrative of hatred and division that was so evident in the United States and abroad.

Soon, Barrio Blues Press produced *Nation* (October 2020) a poetry anthology where Misael Juarez submitted his work. That first collection had poets and artists grapple with how they defined or hoped to define *their* nation. Then, came *Unity, Volume 1: A Magical Realism Anthology* (December 2020), a wonderful volume with over 50 contributing artists, poets, and writers. *Wolf Trek: A Post-Apocalyptic Novelette* (January 2021), a second edition of my own, followed.

The plan was to release at least one anthology a year, maybe a few books here and there. To offer individual contracts for authors was a far-off goal, one I hoped to achieve when I retired in the decades to come, but life has a way of gifting us what we need most.

Like many, the pandemic helped people prioritize what truly mattered. What dreams were worth pursuing? Why wait to live fully? Life was and indeed could be too short. Early in the pandemic (a global crisis that still continues) the pain of loss and fear of death were visceral and ever constant, but they forced me to reconsider my priorities and the future of the press.

When Misael Juarez approached me with a poetry manuscript, I didn't hesitate to accept the offer. I knew from his submissions to *Nation* and getting to know him via Facebook that he was the perfect author for Barrio Blue Press.

Misael Juarez embodies everything this press represents. He is a visionary that wants a better world for chavas and vatos, for the members of his barrio from East Los and his Zapotec community in Oaxaca, México. His dreams for a better world are far-reaching and critical today. The metaphor of poetry, personified as a wife, is deeply moving. For Juarez, that relationship runs deep, and the beauty and intensity he shares is like no other. I would be remiss, if I didn't comment on the healing nature of this book and the uplifting messages directed at people that suffer from mental illness. Though that topic can be taboo in Mexican and LatinX communities, Juarez throws open the curtains for people to see and humanize conditions that should never be stigmatized—that our own barrio gente should neither be ashamed of their psychological wounds, nor ignore them. Instead, our gente should accept them; according to Juarez, they can even be blessings. In that regard, this poetry collection offers something still needed for the people.

It has been a joy to work with Juarez from the beginning stages to the final production of this book. I am proud and honored to present: *My Spoken Word Wife: Playing for Keeps* and Barrio Blues' first contracted author, Misael Juarez.

Finally, a note on language. For the use of italics and Spanish words, often whether to italicize or translate is a political act, especially from Spanish speakers who want to validate their language in the United States. Therefore, I often left the Spanish as part of the English work, without distinguishing the Spanish as something different. It was italicized only when the poet wanted it to be, for a rich complexity that did justice to all the collection. After all, in barrios across the world, the people speak in multiple tongues and don't prioritize one language over the other.

Barrio Blues Press is also a charity press, and it moves me that Misael Juarez has agreed to give the royalties to the League of Revolutionaries for a New America (L.R.N.A.) organization which has the mission to unite revolutionaries and educate Americans on the real possibility of creating a cooperative society, if, like Juarez, we all fight for the futures we deserve.

Introduction

Misael Juarez

My Spoken Word Wife is a collection of stories within poetic structures and rhyme schemes. They honor relationships and romantic experiences. The book is a dedication to the spirit of creativity for allowing me to explore my passion for observing social dysfunction and using my platform for social justice.

Let me explain how the book came to be.

I am a schizophrenic. In Western cultures' psychiatry, schizophrenia is a mental disease, hearing and seeing things that others don't. To me this term is about dealing with otherworldly phenomena, the strange and bizarre. Call it the world of spirit if you must, but it is a real experience characterized as legit by indigenous societies.

I encountered schizophrenia at the age of 17 years old, after being stabbed three times in the back amidst an outbreak of violence in Los Angeles in October 2001. After surgery to stop the internal bleeding, I left the hospital with over 50 staples in my body, and a new ability to hear auditory hallucinations. They became intense in my 20s, eventually consuming my mental capacity until I was unable to dwell on anything else. But I was not diagnosed as schizophrenic until my early 30s.

I began this journey as a member of a gang. A gang that got into trouble because of the poverty around us and the lack of real elders and community support. But through hard work, some of my gang learned to become working class people, painters, soldiers, teachers, poets, and world travelers who served humanity by staying out of trouble.

My poetry writing started on 3rd and Harvard St. and unlike many stories you hear of gangs, my transformation into social justice was supported by my peers, and when all other communities decided to cut me off due to schizophrenia, they stood with me along with my mother and family.

I cannot stress enough the importance of such a community. We were the gang that had no clue how lucky we were to survive our initiation into manhood but were fortunate to learn on our own that it's better to care for family and friends by being responsible. Where some only see a stereotype for lack of better experiences, I see a tribe of warriors who became smart enough to follow their hearts. I cannot talk about *My Spoken Word Wife* without mentioning my origins as a gang member that became interested in the humanities and social justice cause for a world freed from poverty.

At 19 years old, I left a dark, deadly gang path and was able to channel all that street energy and social confusion into an intellectual and creative path by being accepted into a university special admissions program. Before the voices became intense, part of me got into social justice during my early 20s. After reading books and having mentors and teachers at the California State University of Los Angeles, I became solid enough to choose a path of revolutionary ideology, a path seeking to transform a better situation for troubled poor youth, particularly those without the foundation of a supporting education system.

It seemed my path was promising as I even got to work with Civil Rights icon Dr. Robert P. Moses, who taught me a thing or two about social justice and mathematics and being grassroots. I also became a peer supplemental instructor for incoming freshmen at C.S.U.L.A. I was always involved in doing fine promising work, but I had to balance my old pain as a youth, my revolutionary activity, my academics, and my psychotic episodes as they would take me into a strange place and mental state. Although I spent years at the university, I was not able to finish school.

It was in my time alone that I dwelled in the dream world and spent time with the voices of those who did not have a face or mouth. I had the audacity to follow the ancestors into repetitive trouble. The more I followed the ancestral voices, the more alone I became. During my solitude, I began to remember what I was longing for, what I was made of. I remembered that I was made up of a promise to help all those barrio children. But my task during solitude was to break free of those invisible chains, to break free from the frequencies that kept me bound to danger, to reignite my passion for social justice—not the artificial justice, but to get into the revolutionary spirit again.

I realize through writing, a subtle easiness, a more careful observation of life and its details. The poetry I write gives me peace of mind; it's a collaboration between me and the voices. Peace of mind only came as I wrote poetry. The spirit of creativity blessed me with a way to use writing as a practice for dealing with the voices.

By taking the cue from the works of Sir Philip Sydney's Astophel and Stella, and Petrarch's The Canzoniere, two bodies of work that influenced the European Renaissance, I was able to dream my own poetic revolution and love journey that sprang out from my audio hallucinations or spirit guidance. In a parallel universe, it is possible to have guidance to write a poetry book with otherworldly influence. *My Spoken Word Wife* was conceived as voices told me about her existence.

Through writing, I found myself with the creative spirit, picking up the revolutionary and poetic path I detoured from. I learned that in a parallel universe an indigenous scientist can analyze my situation with otherworldly voices as a gift for the world. It is through collaborating with auditory and visual hallucinations that a rhymed mosaic expression for social justice came to be. My past reinforced my attitude to complete my collection of poems. The small amount of support for my revolutionary transformation was enough to bring me out of a poetic and psychedelic cocoon. In this sense, writing served me as a vehicle to relay a message formulated somewhere in between my mind and time and space.

Through psychedelic writing therapy, I have experienced a being who dwells in my heart. I call her my *Spoken Word Wife*, she calls me her Lyrical Husband.

"Her Multiverse" (excerpt)
My Spoken Word Wife came to me in a night's dream
She came from another dimension clearing scenes
Telling me to wordplay and play for keeps all day
We're separated by reality and blue haze

Says she's always been my lovely Spoken Word Wife
She's a galactic empress that purifies life
She exists in a different light reality
She channels through women that are so sweet to me

My Spoken Word Wife is a revolutionary love journey. Through analyzing my relationships with women using poetry, I am able to see that my Spoken Word Wife is a poetic symbol characterized through the women who have blessed me in previous relationships. I look forward to seeing how I will express myself in future writings and how my relationship with her will be further down the road. Enjoy the scenic, wild, street, romantic, and revolutionary journey known as *My Spoken Word Wife: Playing for Keeps.*

My Spoken Word Wife

She's a beautiful brown petite woman
Bringing out my humor and wit full of wisdom
I'm speaking about the poetic barrio goddess
She rules my heart and brings out loving comments

I'm inspired by her soulful loving nature
Pleasing her with words that spell out raw danger
And writing about her bright world is easy
Every word filled with light bringing her home to me

Yet sometimes the world spins like an oldie record
And she's a chola singing through stormy weather
I never surrender to her imperfection
I'm surrendering to her will as a blessing

I penetrate the world with an infinite look
She purposely looks like a dork with a book
While I'm planting a tree in every neighborhood
Making it up to nature for the paper she took

Her world like a still soft and sweet melody
And like a detective I solve a mystery
I'm on the edge of discovering my real gifts
Seeing my destiny without the crucifix

I hold her hand and I get more respect

Forever like this book is my mistress
I see her pain was never meant to be sold
But like the river she is owning true flow

She's the best hand I've ever had so place your bet
Playing my hand like every star depends on it
Her smoke protects me from evil grins
Blowing smoke as I flip the wild aces to win

Living on the edge makes me dangerous
As they give awards for making bold statements
I celebrate her style at L.A. open mics
With this dedication to my Spoken Word Wife

World Star

The rich bourgeois wonder who's my Spoken Word Wife
Raging about the women I've met in my life.
They want to hunt her down and do bad things to her
But I never say who she is to Big Brother.

They wonder if it's that gurl from Telemundo
The woman Mexica dancing so profundo.
Is it the pizza delivery girl who's sweet?
The one behind the cash register that's friendly?

Or the lady with a spin-kick mentality?
The Navy vet with weapons for us to be free
Or professional cheerleader with pom poms.
Or Yalitza Cortez or tortilla honey moms.

Or a porno star lady into the matrix.
Or scuba diver or the mountain climbing Misses
A deported immigrant girl from our country.
The beautiful guerrera with a cash bounty.

Is she a lawyer wearing apple bottom suits?
She's '*no comprendo*' working wearing steel toe boots.
Or a chola applying for minimum wage.
Or Vanessa Guillen's homegurl with a 12 gauge.

She's the math whiz, the fly miss, a cookie baker,
The secretary with files on every hater.
She's the wilderness scout that moves through the whole
    scene.
She's the craziest thing the world has ever seen.

I'll never surrender the info on my gurl.
She's making me create a brand-new world that swirls.
I keep her a secret cause they want her to die
But tu sabes, I love my Spoken Word Wife.

She's a world star doing the most for the people.
She plays for keeps and soars the land of the eagle.
We're deuces gone wild and revolutionary
World stars, hasta la victoria siempre, baby!

Looking Back

My Spoken Word Wife asked me about Harvard Street
It was my barrio fired up for graffiti streaks
We were unique but came from humble beginnings
Like most gangs we sprouted from the Pachuco sins

I kicked it and learned to create street images
Blessing L.A. with street calligraphy pieces
The Harvard Street outlaw mentality rocked scenes
Leaving L.A.P.D. crash units baffling

Cops hired to put us in jail put on a cold show
But marijuana healed our broken-hearted souls
To them we're strong and dangerous to the system
As we behave different with unique wisdom

Racist establishments persecuted our people
We were standing to challenge them like we were made of
    steel
And we rose with brown pride building their hometowns
But why do they manipulate laws to bring us down

Calling us criminal as their heart's pump out fear
They can never truly own our blood sweat or tears
They contract poor kids with school to prison pipelines
But I was tearing up bogus deals with the wolf sign

But before we became a gang, we were taggers
Competing with street crews to see who was badder
I'll paint a picture of what graffiti was like
We weren't bad folk just thrilled boys full of life

I acknowledge all graffiti crews from the 90's
We formed an underground Renaissance for streets
The city paid millions for loss and damages
We were rebels with no money for a canvas

Los Angeles, Zoot Suit Fire 1943

Who's calling the police to stop the madness
News articles are filled with racist passion
Persecuting the Zoot suiters who were poor
But they came uniting the streets during war

I ask the ancestors for permission to ride
Shout out to the big bad Chumash and Tongva tribes
What you know about Broadway named Eternidad?
Cause L.A. was founded by Mexicans and Blacks

My Spoken Word Wife sits and listens to my rhyme
Taking her to moment when young men shined
During the Sleepy Lagoon murder trial signs
Where every L.A. barrio is rooted in time

Cops arrested pachucos for rolling too cool
Because brown dudes were targets for wearing zoot suits
News reporters defamed Chicano young men
Sailors watched growing with a passion to hate them

The navy couldn't stand how pachucos broke rules
A mob of white civilians stormed to ridicule
Teaming up with racist cops to catch them by foot
The pachuco riots set off by white troops

Pachucos were town heroes and city villains
Cops hated the stylish ways of these Mexicans
But creased up Chicano vets always knew laughter
Because these young zoot suiters were word play masters

Trials and tribulations made them wiser
Pachuco riots on streets spread like a wildfire
The servicemen came by the crowds to lose control
Pachucos respected traditions to live bold

Wearing their shiny double stitch shoes on Broadway
Coming from the barrio to shine dance and parlay
In night clubs dressed in silk and wool wearing brim hats
Wooing the pretty women in slacks

Thousands of civilians and servicemen formed mobs
Beating pachucos with weapons to leave them robbed
Stripping off their clothes and shoes while raping women
Black and Asian folk catching blows of racism

Brown, Black, and Yellow beaten throughout old L.A.
It took a truce to unite them to find a way
They became street allies and came up with a plan
Arming up to protect themselves to fight the white man

A neighborhood uprising called them to be free
Racist white cops driving folks to insanity
While the Jews persecuted for their own culture
Pachucos enlisted to be combat soldiers

Calling them animals yet they too fought Nazis

Reppin' for every kid in the barrio and street
The pieces of the story don't always add up
The talk about fighting over fashion and such

Some trace gangbanging back to the Zoot Suit Riots
Only wanting to protect ourselves from hate groups
The pachuco street victory downplayed with lies
But I honor the city's ancestors with pride

Who's calling the police to stop the madness
News articles are filled with racist passion
But pachucos placed their bets on unity
Ending the street riots with a victory

Graffiti Angels 1996

She loves it when I'm hitting up to keep it real
I'm the soul rebel gangster lyrical hero
Schooling these graffiti crews into infantries
To rock city blocks like revolutionaries

City hall calls for curfews to control the youth
Scared of giant letters from street tagging crews
I write about the times with metaphors and rhymes
Speaking truth to power making y'all press rewind

Tagged out corporate signs are great lyric topics
Knowing in graffiti streets banks cannot profit
C.E.O.s hate removing tagging like I do
But youngsters tag walls like it's so sweet and cool

Injustice plagues the hood, but we seek good trouble
Respecting the streets and our beautiful struggles
Driving past the 10-freeway I see graffiti
And L.A.P.D. wondering if it was me

Hit up my name on the bus stop with acrylic
They incarcerated my peers for doing it
But they couldn't control taggers with tough answers
As Belmont Tunnels were sprayed with so much laughter

Metro bus window displays were ridiculous
That's why company leaders felt so furious
High school students found ways to write on public walls
Out of nowhere graffiti galleries stood tall

The player of words mobbed postal stickers on streets
Riding the subway made me bust flows to beats
I came riding on cars catching the summer breeze
Spraying my nickname on the concrete to be free

Some paint logos for profit and have it restored
Taggers took cans and commerce with local paint stores
All the homies searched for visible spots to graff
As cops surveilled while we all laughed

Some wrote on freeways with a colorful rampage
My message for the streets about coming of age
Harvard Street foo's flossed jersey numbers without shame
Graffiti is a game about the best street fame

As aerosol chemistry was left through cities
Mother's prayed for kids in streets with Rosary beads
Gentrification brought rich folks with .44s
Landowners who turned old buildings into condos

Raising the rent on the poor like they are heartless
Developers kicked families out of apartments
New residents scored drugs in their brand-new Jaguars
Crying the city is full of graffiti wars

And taggers from L.A. were some of the baddest

We were rebels with no money for a canvas
Flossing our black book pieces with silver and gold
That's how we showed the City of Angels our soul

Aerosol Girl

She wears a pink hoodie and lime green shoes
With long hair braids she's an apple bottom jean muse
Standing over milk crates to graffiti brick walls
Coloring block letters with hearts that never fall

She hopped on a moving old city bus bumper
Held on tight and spray painted her name in wonder
She was arrested and fined, but she kept tagging
And broke every law to follow her life's passion

Her rivals were graffiti boys who flared spray paint
Competing against gambits with their fingers taint
Corporate advertisements don't last a long time
She can steal their show by tagging up signs

Police look for acrylic paint on her hands
They shined bright lights on her face and left her to stand
Padding her down while grabbing her breast like bastards
But she moaned to clown and gave her crew laughter

I saw her arrested—became a lonely drunk
Angry with the system the city acts like punks
Cops aren't the answer teens condemned and Damned
She even tagged up streets forbidden by big gangs

Someone is kidnapping indigenous women
She hit the streets to alert us with raw wisdom
Representing graffiti tribes and their gambits
Dodging Ralph Perez and corrupt Rampart badges

She made songs to describe fat aerosol spray tips
How to flare her concepts like letters when she spits
Able to flip street knowledge to the rhythmic beats
She quickly made money and now she leads the streets

The moon is her best friend and the only lighting
She rattles cans—She's bound by guerrilla fighting
She's moving as the streetwise graffiti ninja
When she spray paints her name she hollers at all ya'

Girl from the Block

She woke up 'round noon ran to bathroom to be neat
Went out to defeat goons with the Harvard Street
Peripheral vision to see beyond dead ends
Playing to win getting lit as her day began

About to go near streets where they throw up gang signs
Where young women flaunted their bodies to bump and
  grind
She ran inside the house 'cause she saw the street curse
Pulled out a chrome 45 tuck under her shirt

Pointing the weapon, she schooled them with life lessons
Saying, knock it off you chicken heads keep steppin'
Jumped in the blue civic flared the engine right up
She scraped the Honda as she took flight up the block

Smoking a cigarette, she rolled down her window
A pimp blew a kiss she blew smoke back at his soul
The economic battle made her pack heat
But the justice system was corrupt to pull teeth

She passed by the liquor store near the hot corner
A junky opened the door and asked for quarters
She gave him a dollar and he put it away
Vatos from around the way approached with a sway

She said she ain't fun to be with under the sun
They was gonna talk shit but she flashed the gun
Then I saw them leaving in a Mercedes Benz
She saw me and gave me a cold brew cause we friends

She said something to me that I couldn't believe
That she wanted to join that crazy Harvard Street
Reached back for my bag pulled out a notebook with
    psalms
And asked her if she could sing the hook to a song

Subterranean L.A. Street Deuce

She's in the basement plays my mixtape 'till the end
I'm on the pavement talking 'bout the reptilians
She wears a hoodie reading *The People's Tribune*
She has a recipe for a wooden stick broom

Lookout girl, somethin' 'bout selling weed cigarettes
Cops don't let go when they choke grip and stage arrest
She better hit the chain fence with her old blue Vans
Down the alley avoiding those in the white van

Surrounded by homegirls talkin' bout the dance hall
One needs a ride to bail out her bro who just called
"The phone's tapped anyway." She says her car's bad
Says her creep neighbor would fix that if he could hit 'that'

"Don't matter what you do. They'll still call you Bimbo"
They say betta' stay cutthroat, aim for a combo
How 'bout you record that mixtape on the cell phone
She says, "Rather use a mic and hear the base Boom"

Rain drops falling, it's time to go home with her luck
A wino hollers at them, they spare a cash buck
They get approached by a tamalera vendor
She buys tamales for her abuela at work

Look out, kid, there's an incoming pimp walking by

Has a Rolex mocking the simp that pays for nights
Hangs 'round the beach by the concrete stairs with a flare
Lookin' for a new fool, acting with a cold stare

"I got direction with full protection," he says.
"I'm about the 4 directions," she states with faith
A woman walks handing her pimp fast made money
She yells, "Don't fuck with a revolutionary."

Look out, kid, he signals a hit from a crackhead
But she packs a chrome 45 for those mob debts
They throw away the knives and turn red in the face
I show up and drive her to a place where she's safe

La Pachucada

She has ink tattoos that read life gets easier
Her Kung Fu spin kicks make her a hardcore sister
She's the woman in the mirror breaking it down
Through the looking glass she enters with sonic sound

The lady zoot suiter plagues police computers
She's Carmen San Diego with magic elixirs
From the crazy westside to eastside boulevard
She's time traveling in a classic bomba car

Treating the players club like couch potatoes
Smoking from her wooden pipe she lets go smoke
Blasting enemies while schooling little homies
Recording herself singing to classic oldies

She became America's number 1 stunner
Praying with good deeds because actions speak louder
But she's wanted dead or alive by the fascist
They want her gifts and talents but life's about risk

She can dance the jitterbug just to pay homage
Escape from evil setups with kicks and punches
La pachucada and her brown suede coat enchant
With a robin bird's feather on her black brim hat

She understands life's trouble and goes full throttle
The spirit's double o' seven Kim Possible
They hide their evil like demonic masterminds
She outsmarts the devil's advocates with slick rhymes

She can take a phrase and rhyme it with her sayings
Record it where it would be played at Lover's Lane
Mold you with her dynamic static to rove hills
Counting the stars like syllables with love that's real

The forces of adversity hit a dead end
She came in with dual guns and left behind dead men
I ran into her, and it was good to catch up
She bought me a cup of coffee to show me love

Keep Ya' Head Up

I know a hot fire will soothe your broken heart
The moon over mountains inspires our deepest thoughts
While brown women bake brown adobe pottery
Beautiful grandmas talk revolution and seeds

As even our own people dim our life with lies
We honor ancestors and take soul flights with light
But sweetheart don't weep don't you cry never give up
Reality is dead while our dreams soar above

And when they claim you are nothing don't believe them
Without us they would be living in oblivion
Mija, keep your chin up and level the score
Play your cards right and do it as an act of war

But know what makes me unhappy—is how bros die
Killing their own folk while supporting the white hype
And since we all came from a beautiful woman
I wonder why they betrayed grandfather's wisdom
Time to be legit with the wise who cares

Time to make a choice and raise your fist in the air
So when the real scout shows up I know you'll bless him
But please praise the fierce protector and play to Win

I remember Cantinflas used to clown with dreams
Had me thinking I'll be a street wordplaying king
Suddenly the barrio came alive with the mic
And though we had it tough we double checked our rights

Huffed and puffed about curfews and broken rules
Ran with the Harvard crew mobbing the streets with truth
I realized my family earned their stripes to fight
Bound together while honoring an ancient flight

As working poor folk, paying the price to live right
Coming up to raise our children with a sense of pride
All I had to do is play my cards with the mic
Made foes fold their bet if they wanna test my might

I was making dollars out of rhyming with my best
Being legit with wordplay as I stood the rest
Seemed like I was heading all the way to the top spot
Had very few friends show me love when the fun stopped

Last night I lost my grandfather and said goodbye
He taught me to win hearts without buying the lies
It's gonna take blessings to make it to the stage
Rain don't stop in a jungle where it pours like rage

You know it's funny when it rains it pours
They make us pay for their war to enslave the poor
We ain't meant to survive, 'cause it's all a set-up

And despite being fed up, keep ya' head up

To every man working to provide for their kids
I know it gets hard when the law gets in ya' bizz
Changing your game plan to do right with low wages
Back to slanging rocks instead of writing on the pages

Momma stressed over bills and can't take it no more
Looking at dudes with a Rolex that play the poor
But you too upset to talk it out, so you bang
Caught up in trial 'stead of holding your kid's hand

You can't complain for feeling broken and helpless
3 kids hurt cause they're father is disrespected
While you were trying to do something for the better
The rich man got a quick fix and then left her

The boys are growing with the taste of uselessness
Not enough done to unite in togetherness
While her heart aches she finds her old soulmate
A young boy saying keep your head up pretty babe

Love at Union Station

The M.T.A. bus hauled through traffic like a snail
And I boarded after leaving the county jail
I was young and lost in a terrible system
So, the bus driver let me on without payment

It came to a halt when a passenger pressed the bell
She stepped inside holding her brand new cell
Didn't have the confidence to show my phone
Technology disqualifies the best men home

I felt like making a movie out the whole scene
As the world opened up like a summertime dream
She was on social media promoting events
I thought she must have been heaven sent

We got off at the old L.A. Union Station
I walked with her to the next stop and listened
I wonder how she grew courageous with wordplay
She talked to the moon in her writing everyday

While she recited a poem about scandals
Poems about justice and rights to land for all
She drew pure wisdom from my legal trials
She never met an attentive wild street vato
My alternate views made her see me different

An instant crush, a feeling so vibrant
Seeing her by the light of the unchained me
She's smart pure loving sweet like golden honey

A blue jay landed to eat the crumbs from the floor
I saw it as a sign that she nourished my soul
Perhaps I made my mistakes to wind up here
I listened to her wordplay she spits without fear

She laughed at my jokes pleased with my fast wit
We exchanged phone numbers and our day ended lit
Drawing inspiration from her dreamlike verbs
I began writing with light to honor such words

Sunset Rhymes

The flower on her hair matches her summer dress
As she blesses us with a compassionate verse
She uses profound imagery in her rhymes
Describing the town with metaphorical lines

There's a red rose under the sunset taking shape
She's rhyming over beats found in old cassette tapes
Reciting over a fire pit filled with red coals
The audience clap their hands to the rhythm and flow

A rose is a trumpet of the earth that can cleanse
Where nature's sound explodes in magical silence
The two complement one another's existence
One is lyrical the other—great abundance

She's an exotic emcee with sweet mystery
Her honeycomb thoughts are revolutionary
Her hummingbird volcanic vocabulary
Rhyming for her rights as a free young lady

She's a poet of the people and the city
I tease her to make her bright as a daisy
She responds with mezcal shots and says I'm crazy
I don't say it out loud, but it doesn't phase me

I stay clever to jump in the mix and freestyle
Staying on time on point with grace and style
Rocking like jagged cliffs using humor and wit
Kicking melodies with knowledge I emit

Making money by owning the language is key
Every dead poet dreamed of pimping melodies
But she flashes a phrase like sweet advertisements
Selling her new poetry book for cash payments

I eat a juicy piece of cooked steak off the grill
She keeps eyeing me with a fiery sexy chill
And at the end of the night, we're loving easy
Intoxicated with poetic chemistry

My Apartment

Understand crime waves reflect the economy
People risk prison time for hungry mouths to feed
Gambling with your freedom gets old
School to prison pipelines are sad and cold

Police choppers are high over roofs flashing beams
Searching for a brother portrayed as a crack fiend
The corporate media is here making us seem
Like city criminals all in one scene

My girlfriend holds her purse and a bottle of wine
We are walking past the yellow caution tape lines
I have a bag full of books for my school classes
Ready to write an essay bout' Aztecs

A cop checks ID, so we can enter the block
My neighbor with audacity to smoke crack rock-
While being illegal in the country waves hi
Detectives take pictures of street vibes and take flight

She enters my apartment, she lets her hair down,
"I'm in the mood to drink some wine and leave this
And despite being fed town."
I reply, "Capitalism is everywhere, hon'."
"Right. There's microcosms everywhere," she reasons.

She vents for about an hour, and I just listen
"Ey . . . are you even still listening?" She questions
I say, "I am, but I'm tired" and lay down in bed
"Corazón." She lays next to me to rest her head

"I love when you're clear as a night after the rain.
But something tells me we too old to play this game
We either spend it getting creative or lame
'Cause we're sitting ducks if we don't spark a new flame."

I was used to her long talks about tomorrow
She drank about a third of her red wine bottle
The night was warm the hard issues became amends
Her words becoming moans in my apartment

Summertime

Born in the City of Angels with the lightning
She kisses me with red lipstick while I'm driving
Styling sitting shotgun chewing on bubblegum
Her sunglasses and earrings dangle freedom

A penny for every time we seen graffiti
A dime for every piece of chewing gum in streets
A quarter for every kid with a freestyle rap
I'd have enough to buy my own navy aircraft

Street graffiti mural with Frida Kahlo's face
Next to barrio names on walls during summer days
The sunset makes her take a photo of the wall
A wall screaming insane in the brain to us all

Chevy impalas cut the corner like they soar
But I'm driving a bucket full of dreams to score
It's all about shining with a vibe that's correct
It's the way I'm driving that earned her respect

Economic leaps leave behind scrapped cars
It takes an artist to flip the value with art
It takes maintenance and investment to drive far
Treat the revolution like the road play it smart

She's elegant snapping photos of the city
Capturing time and place gruesome realities
She snaps a bird's heartbeat before its flight
Changing landscapes and streetlight poles in the twilight

I think about what a camera can hold
To have a gallery with pictures being sold
To inspire new consciousness and poetic verse
To examine moments and see the universe

Still life can move people from the correct angle
People either see homeless people or angels
Making life appear mysterious as life lessons
Never once took a picture of her sweet wisdom

Up by the River

This pretty lady has curves like the clear river
She speaks with rhythm in verse as a good leader
Running game with cool waters in the hot season
Her rebel elegance holds up canyon wisdom

She's chanting for the wolf to near the river creek
Moving water with her spoken word poetry
Revolutionaries must adapt to our souls
It's our souls that shift the movement to be bold

Her ranchera straw hat and tight blue fitted jeans
Go well with her tank top, sandals, and golden rings
Her voice gives me instructions to move in easy
To tell the water that I need her to kiss me

She divines my emcee game with white cowrie shells
Speaks about living with poetic business sales
Saying that I shall play for keeps and protect youth
Show them how to cash in their words in studio booths

She takes honey and milk and pours it on water
She cleanses my head in the river to sense power
I emerge in her care and beautiful prayers
Says my destiny is to be a wordplayer

Though revolution will not be televised by them,
It will be mocked by bad movies and viral trends
She goes on, "A poet can break fast with the light,
But the street rapper can blaze the path with the mic."

I get up and relieved of the heavy burdens
Relieved of the social pressure that I'm stirred in
I say, "Thank you," and she replies with a wet kiss
Saying, "Corazón, how does my warrior like this?"

"It's up to the man upstairs if I should soar or die,
If I should kiss you and fly over the blue sky."
She replies, "Missing you is like a bad fever."
I say to her the truth is I'll always seek her

Like High Voltage

She be cultivating *maíz* like high voltage
Flossing Zapata signs at the city collage
The ancestors fight racist ideologies
Throwing up the X with our arms as memories

Dreaming of flowing like a blue river on stage
But she chooses to nourish young children with sage
Laughs at capitalists trying to keep her down
She's too wild and free to even frown around town

A curandera using bright syntax with caps
Capping playa-haters like bottles till they're flat
Just know we capping them all off with fire and smoke
Then turn to the golden honey sun joke

Willing and able to turn the tables around,
Flip cards over till they're jokers are upside down
She reads the cards like tarot charging them up
Revealing past and future moves to call their bluff

Economies demand high tech machinery
It's either that or they demand wage slavery
But she's been misplaced, she's an outcast in a way
The system is afraid of her poetic sway

Graffiti is a sign that there's more folk like her
Speaking to the masses with a sharp tongue street verse
She's badass with the ink pen writing poetry
Searching heartaches for beauty under an oak tree

I tell her love is abstract, see it as easy
Making money is legit when you rock the beat
Only dumb women agonize for direction
I'm standing like a sign for future instruction

She's taller for having a dream bucket list upfront
Always keeping herself preserved like a love font
If she were a phrase, she would read something like this:
Kiss me with everything you got for my sweet bliss

Play Your Cards Right

War makes everyone cringe at the sight of terror
A revolutionary responds with flavor
Words written on paper give it value and worth
Use a mic and make the crow roar with metaphors

She's analyzing the times for contradictions
Social media lets you in, everyone can't win
Your profile gives you a platform to learn a thing
Learn to shift conversations by imagining

She questions institutions and politicians
For every bomb dropped she rhymes lines as her mission
They incarcerate immigrants with tax money
Freedom is a luxury—Everyone ain't free

She be playing her cards right without sabotage
Focused on bright dreams instead of an entourage
Shuffling the card deck without looking at the cards
A set of cards for players from the boulevard

The system can be out hustled by the good folk
Every player plugged in the system can be woke
The sleeping giant tosses and turns till awakened
Noticing the dawn when it's done pissin' the can

She be counting the Queens and Kings for trouble
Understanding many get lost in the shuffle
Her keen eye detects them hidden under a sleeve
Or marked by a scratch when they're in need by the greed

Nobody teaches you the right way to be great
You make choices and bet your own winnings at stake
The physical gets old and wears down everyday
Only your light and spirit can provide better ways

She's like a sweet pearl from the oyster down under
It wasn't till I went soul deep that I found her
Counting the political cards on the table
When they wage war it's always to fake freedom moves

L.A. Artist

They raise the cost of living but not our wages
I'm a schizophrenic dreaming of world stages
Passing by upper class folks sipping hot coffee
Near the downtown L.A. skid row streets where folks sleep

The woman I'm with tolerates my situation
She understands the economy lacks wisdom
But she adapts easy cause she's secure with love
It's easy transforming scenes as two turtle doves

Beneath Santa Monica Pier with a sandwich
I wonder if they know how cold the homeless live
My companion breathes a soulful revolution
Clears confusion regardless of retribution

Having a thing call schizophrenia is a path
Searching for the heart of the city with a laugh
I wonder how some of us see it different
We hustle making money paying bills and rent

Economies are polarized dividing folk
Each one can't survive without the other so close
'Takes sacrificing comfort to be side by side
But society builds walls to hide facts and lies

She gets to see me grow while I rock hip hop shows
I'm blasting rap music through an amp when I flow
Chasing my dreams like city cops to bank robbers
Ain't locking them up, but setting them free as workers

The world can't spin without the harmony keepers
We must give of ourselves to make our life sweeter
Nothing can buy your hurt or exploit it with cash
It takes sobering thoughts to walk straight with a laugh

She made my world better with sincere compassion
We're organizing the next gigs with more action
The world is a situation that can be survived
But why stop there—We must go achieve something wise

Made for Rap

Los Angeles is known for jails and poverty
And full of light with wisdom and epic stories
I see those hard-working people without the fear
Making this country great with their blood, sweat, and
  tears

But these times call us to be real brave in the heart
'Cause L.A.P.D. has been too rough acting hard
Police are angry at everyone with brown love
Exploiting power, swearing they have a tough job

Let it be known that this country is war hungry
And our U.S. troops suffer when they die lonely
It's expensive to support the habits of the rich
They hoard wealth while ignoring the impoverished

They persecute brown children like it's patriotic
Spirit protects them as static and dynamic
I'm a street vet riding for my childhood dreams
Living on the edge with comrades rocking the scene

I got to get up quick to survive the madness
As my vision makes me a survivor at best
I been at the bottom to rise like tidal waves
Clearing energy that gave me so much heartbreak

I make my offerings to ancestors who watch
With a smile giving gratitude for what I've got
I'm so into my Spoken Word Wife when I rise
But I have to leave her when it's time to go ride

Being brave in the heart for my kids to grow up
Show me a starting line, and I will finish off
My style is something enemies praise like a dream
Defeating adversity cause I am a king

Returning back home after being stranded at sea
Rocking metaphors like they are my golden fleece
The word doctor brings the Jedi verse like a bomb
Cause my double speakers blast when they play my song

Revolutionary Dreams

So, I never look back or down on my bad luck
It's never late to write a flight for sitting ducks
But if the economy wishes automation
Then, we're mighty ducks to ask for revolution

I'm riding for the fallen graffiti artists
Honoring dreamers with hip-hop hits that uplift
The world persecutes the street poet and artist
When they try to pass racist laws that are fascist

The corporate media speaks nonsense about us
Blaming gangbangers for rotting the city buzz
And then turn to exploit our street gangster wisdom
But we view diamonds like a curse on poor children

While some think they have it all they walk in the dark
To shine on the streets, you must have courage and heart
Staying pure like brown children extracting cocaine
Born to rebel freeing their villages from pain

While most rappers don't challenge the cruel injustice
My rhymes slap up the system with raw messages
Cause if you're homeless rapping on the boulevard
Know that being skilled takes practicing hip hop bars

When I take a chance, the tools are in place to go

Fans surround the stage like it's made of gold soul
The world spins as the DJ plays old school records
I start to rap with the mic like a go-getter

She can smile and break a curse on me with pure love
Knew it all along that heaven paid me a dove
Changing the economy with my poetry
Has me writing my verse simply for unity

She's wearing an ocean blue dress with bright sparkles
Dancing under stage lights, we drop the hottest flow
Being photographed by a hip hop magazine
We bomb the scene with revolutionary dreams

Breathtaking Gal

I asked her for her name, and I felt connected
Her dangerous curves had me swerve feeling lifted
Women break cycles of capitalist madness
Every time they wordplay as the rebel gambits

She's enticing when she's rhyming with blue lightning
Flashing a light on economical fighting
The war between rich and poor folk hasn't ended
The poor do the work but never understand it

She came through the black door and took me to the top
Changing lanes like we own the road and the pit stop
We came far traveling further into the mist
Searching for the elixir and soulful uplifts

With more bounce to the ounce is my poetic flow
She's my number 1 when it comes to rocking shows
We keep our cards out of plain sight because it's right
Taking people from movement into greater heights

How to unite a world divided by borders?
Every economy has its darkest corners
Not everyone has a mattress to get some sleep
'Cause they are darkening first world nations with greed

She's yearning for a melody to start rhyming
She rocks the mic right and rides with the blue lightning
She's the one mic, street poet, spin' ya ear canals
Soul shaking, rhyme saying, sweetheart—breathtaking gal

The wages to be a rhyme sayer are gracious
While love and revolution makes her audacious
I sly to sweep her off her feet with the rhythm
Making ends meet using words filled with raw wisdom

From a small-time pen pal to when the rap beat calls
Amazing critics and naysayers see her ball
She's the one mic, street poet, spin ya' ear canals
Soul shaking, rhyme saying, sweetheart—breathtaking gal

The Young Vato with Enormous Wings

She reminds women to shift their focus on life
That being unfortunate can earn you the stripes
We're stats from police roulette and punishment hype
A system meant to divide families must die

The crisis crushing society is the prisons
Families broken by unforgiving systems
She reminds me to be courageous and wise
Everyone in jail can fight with a new pair of eyes

The radio plays "Angel Baby" that sweet oldie!
My beautiful gal sings wearing a black hoodie
Her hoop earrings dangle to a boulevard dream
The bright crescent moon laughs like an old barrio queen!

Her dangerous curves are paved by day laborers
The storm rider swerves to land on her ear with words
Bringing a white flower from her neighbors garden
Has her heart vibing through her lips like an arson

While her eyes sparkle like the stars are breathing air
The coal embers in my chest ignite with a dare
I tell her soft, "Take my hand and never let go"
Kissing me she says, "I love your barrio blues soul!"

I say, "You're my brown sugar and cup of coffee."
She laughs, "No wonder you're so alert and so sweet."
"You're like a chola sin barrio," I tease again,
"But your barrio is of spirit and the four winds."

I say, "I'm into our moments but this paper
Ain't stacking itself, I must focus my labor."
She puts her arms 'round my neck and says, "We have
    dreams
Ain't no good if we starve—We must balance the scene"

We leave the house and enter the pandemic scene
This that raw 'love in the time of Covid-19'
She laughs and says, "In my barrio version of things,
You're more like the young vato with enormous wings."

Like It's Witchcraft

She's the emcee who writes it down like it's witchcraft
When she licks her lips softening a vocab crash—
It's like hearing waves rolling onto Cali shores
But I'm the daring surfer with the boogie board

If I ever meet destiny, she'd spit like that
I want her to scream and shout my name when I rap
I'm on the great quest to get more bounce to the ounce
But watching 3 orcas whales rise had me wiped out

Some folks who act like my comrades are ruthless villains
Just cause we're from the Harvard Street cold chillin'
And her cool story contains glory and thunder
Because I delivered the craziest number

She sits at home smoking, wearing just pantyhose
Exploring a game of wits, that's a life hustle
We play lyrical chess and checkers having fun
Eyeing my every move with a cold daring response

She's street poetry, a shooting star, and much more
We're the poets engaging in gun battle wars
When we ride we light up the night with metaphors
But her honey words knock me out to fly and soar

The revolution blessed us with strong alchemy
Blocking magic to be fast against enemies
Defeating the odds with a sweet praise to God's work
But we're smoking peyote with Huichol masters

They're trying to install fear till we're all trembling
But fear is not of this earth, so we're battling
Cause we're heroic philosophers and warriors
Bombing their concepts with kinetic static words

She's gifted to place her bet on the man she loves
Gambling with the sixth sense to soar high up above
With her on my team makes me see that I'm so blessed
We recite for all the children who live oppressed

On Her Politics

I slang rhymes like a street mystic, make cash and bounce
Say things without saying it honoring my crown
Lifting spirits up with DJs and a chrome mic
But I must sing of a sweet woman who is wise

She works hard and pays taxes like everyone else
Understanding wealthy folks keep most of their wealth
She questions why the poor pay more taxes to live—
The rich get tax breaks and special federal lifts

She's a pretty face emcee but talks like she's wild
Above the law when judges break oaths on Bibles
Studying arguments for social policies
She has a movement backing up her poetry

When the powers that be persecute her with spite,
She fights with coherent ideas that are bright
Moving conversations with the rhythm and beat
Focusing everyone with all her dignity

Economies are a social construct of man
Only caring people can make us understand-
That our society needs leaders with good hearts
It takes people to recognize good folks to start

She rolls her r's like dice mix with sugar and spice

Poetry is a tax on political lies
She's the I.R.S. of truths to be spoken soft
Every time I get rowdy she says, "Add more love."

If she has a clear path it's 'cause she's protected
Only her faith tells us how to comprehend it
Some women are never found in the card shuffle
Lost while card players wait for them to go hustle

Taking remains of a tree to make arts and crafts
Nothing can go to waste, things must be loved to last
People kill for meat forgetting everything else
Seeing we're in trouble if we focus on wealth

Queen of Hearts

A guitar amp follows her delivery pace
As she honors her mother's struggles with raw grace
She takes her words and dazzles like star shatter nights
Making the summer open mic slam a delight

Shooting for the stars under a blue fiery moon
Telling class stories about a country consumed
Capitalism makes profit off a dead corpse
War is the shadiest cash money metaphor

She recites to the percussion and melody
Landing her street verse like fist of jaguar fury
She can open her periphery to scout ghosts
Track energy and confusion fast like thunder bolts

She uses her ambition with boss player deuce
And as the queen of hearts, she's respected by rules
Playing her hand with her sincere heart on her sleeve
Speaking the sea language using her poetry

War makes children fatherless, and wives grieve their hurt
If it wasn't for the rich people's gluttonous work-
The world would be free truly ready to evolve
Riches never align with the loving earth gods

Her emotions sweep like Pacific Ocean tides
Clearing pain and shame from sand tracks and stolen lives
Folk howl after hearing her delicious phrases
As if folk's souls are fed by how she amazes

Dollars calculate their way towards her business
She's known for her service that gave her cool sweetness
She accessed a network only grassroots folk can
Making profit from word of mouth with a good plan

She never breaks down during a bad match of wits
Bringing revolutionary feminine lifts
Challenging the status quo and cold world with sparks
Making time unwind standing as the queen of hearts

Playing for Keeps

It's the Chicano gambit blowing white smoke
With my beautiful babe telling fun jokes
She's never weeping for love cause I'm next to her
Keeping her in the mood, shifting our love like birds

The seasoned veteran with rebel elegance
Compare a chain link fence as a property grin
Land equals opportunity for the village
But the price is too high when they come and pillage

She has me studying words with fluidity
The verbs in my verse must agree with unity-
Or she'll clown around and break me down to the teeth
It takes a carefree poet to rock the street beat

The game can be played dirty with a spell and hex
She's always washing her cards to respect the next
Praying for protection is what players should do
Paying respect for the card dealer being true

The lessons from the streets to government pulpits
What they can't handle with words they solve with bullets
It's a calling for all men who walk in prayer
Witness the wordplayer rise as the mic slayer

She's telling me softly she's on a winning streak
The bartender brings us drinks, we're not for slur speech
She's all in and winks at me like a playful sign
The whole table is out the game in a short time

For some folk, luck is a mystery, a fire sign
Luck is a thing people say to explain the grind,
Hustle for pennies changes to more and plenty
We shift into an abundant mentality

But we've encountered strange beings against our luck
As we're playing for keeps like we don't give a fuck
Keepin' her in my vista with love that's crazy
Saying, hasta la victoria siempre baby!

Capture the Ocean

I'm inspired by revolutionary nature
Sharper than a flint knapped stone knife made for danger
I'm the wilderness scout and soul adventurer
The wolf entering her heart like a tomb raider

She's a curandera but also the sweetest
I kick it with her and her red candy kisses
Shooting truths like a chrome gun with rebellious words
Fighting for freedom and land with every gun burst

Living life with fierce love to take flight over the world
We show compassion for orphan boys and girls
We capture the ocean through poetic wordplay
Forever mine blues and forever and a day

She's the sweet wonder, a phenomenal woman
Ain't no nice guy, I'm the worst with old school wisdom
Penetrating the world with an infinite eye
I'm here playing for keeps and playing my cards right

Chopping wood for the sweat lodge and adobe stove
It's all from nature—my primitive arrows and bow
Using wild edibles to shift my strength and dreams
And it's a must to play for communal settings

She studies poetry like her own beauty marks
Reads Aztec cosmology to mend broken hearts
Ignited her soul with blue lightning and thunder
She rose from the concrete paved by her grandfather

I can exchange work energy for currency
Or tap into the primitive psychology
Never doubt that nature teaches us to be free
To look and capture the ocean like her sweet feet

Ceremony gave me the chance to be so bold
Racing against the powers that be made me grow
Knowing poetic feet can capture the ocean
I studied her foot's track to sense her emotion

The Blue Language

When the world vibrates a musical melody
She's a detective entering great mysteries
Living right on the edge of an infinite world
Smoking sage stone medicine making white smoke swirl

As the stars are pounding on her rooftop at night
Gray wolves appear in her dreams asking her to ride
Delivering barrio gospels to city blocks
Living with the earth staying away from crack-rock

She brings on the cold winter when spitting rare truths
Fading away misconceptions about poor youth
She exposes the subliminal bigotry,
The media's propaganda by the enemy,

Corporate pirates rampaging economies,
The devil's magic binding souls to slavery,
They use debt, meth, and violence to seduce women

But they can't handle her bold renegade wisdom
Black magicians don't love the indigenous children
Hating themselves losing their vision to demons
The capitalist industry tells them that it's cool
But she creates reverb effects against their tools

When the clouds have come, and the world feels a great
    storm
She flows to ignite the night with blue lightning bolts
She's standing tall and strong like thirteen grandmothers
Swaying with the wind as she clears the black waters

Redemption songs heard by revolutionaries
Echo the times that we need to bring in money
We bet our overtime deuce and make up movements
But the hustle and grind are what makes us all win

We live on earth and battle our foes with star light
We are strangers, but we never fake the funk type
We must be alert and awake, the star warriors
Speaking the blue language of the ocean waters

The Raven's Flight

She always brings indigenous beats to the streets
But she's not new to this work releasing the breeze
She's burning words with a Nahuatl dictionary
Delivering alchemy and chemistry

Freeing those who ride with her to the city beat
With a wild child she still knows how to play for keeps
Too raw to respect nothing but a freedom verse
Cause she's way doper than they give her credit for

A sweet praise to Creator with poetic thoughts
Commercial free as we drink for that mezcal buzz
She performs at the bar while the crowd adores her
We listen cause it's gracious to hear her laughter

Her adventurous way to wordplay gets her paid
I can't believe her pretty face ain't on airwaves
Representing beautiful women in prison
The sacred feminine and exploited children

Brighter than the stars on Hollywood Boulevard
Her poems are classic cars that are riding far
Blessing our great City of Angels with wordplay
Moving us with words to live for a better way

Showering crowds with beautiful lyricism
As she lights the stage with beautiful expressions
Such a rare flower blooming in the spring season
Blossom to believe she's on a greater mission

Reciting verses that's making us all addicts—
To her wordplay cause she's dynamic and static
A dynamite emcee lifting a rare rose vibe
Working in a studio where she'll record tonight

Phenomenal woman with true Mexican roots
Representing grassroots and indigenous crews
I've never seen so much beauty from one lady
All I want her to know is she drives me crazy

The Word Doctor's Medicine

I am a man at war with the prison system
On a lyrical mission to free the children
The ancestors teach me how to win victory
My rhymes defeat billionaires and sucker emcees

Riding with the wolves to go and roll on my foes
Unleashing metaphors to rock the beautiful—
Gorgeous, sweet sexy nurse who works to cleanse the hurt
In emergencies where we uplift the street curse

By being true to ancestral roots in the booth
Soaring like the bald eagle with a strong outlook
Over avenues and dark alleys full of scrawl
With dreamers and taggers hitting up names roll call

Standing under the streetlight where we're true and brave
Where we gather to chill cause we just worked all day
We move in stealth playing oldies to ease our mood
As young warriors in a dangerous neighborhood

I'm the lyricist riding with a sweet woman
Dreaming the world into being like a shaman
As her melody soothes me to flow real *suave*
And honor the duende near the sweet agave

Supplying the doctors medicine with the wolf
I'm rocking rhymes in the booth speaking to the youth
Cause freedom songs inspire the young and the restless
With a courageous heart when the world wants to test us

I'm a speeding bullet living to the fullest
Believing I'm breathing to release classic hits
Making money is a curse if you're full of greed
Don't respect billionaires when kids sleep on concrete

The crowd roars at my shows when I let them all know
Fighting injustice provides you with a bold soul
And the word doctor is here to uplift the curse
Bringing a cool sudden breeze when I spit and swerve

Real Crazy and Super Bad

It's an economic situation that's tough
And it's the right time to say I love her so much
The brainiac dealing with maniac alert
Ghetto girls will fall back too if weren't for her

She's thinking of money making 'cause there's a need
Using high tech machinery, she never sleeps
Creating the future with computer keyboards
Playing in the league using software metaphors

I'm staring at her face—She's so fun and loving
Blazing cannabis wondering about money
She comes up with a plan to make cash with a laugh
But to me she sounds real crazy and super bad

Life deals a new set of cards, then you make it work
It's never a bad day when you work with effort
Gratitude helps the workday go fast till it's done
She always reminds me to take the steps and have fun

Replacing human labor without warning ya'
Robotic assembly creeps through America
If robots were public servants, it would be a great day
It takes economic leaders showing the way

She is a beautiful woman who grew up poor
Knowing science and math, having vision to soar
Using communication, able and willing
She rises and levels up breaking through glass ceilings

I play to win even if I ain't playing cards
I have to give her the chance to test out her smarts
Using math as a tool, she multiplies earnings
Creating a percentage for retirement dreams

She takes her grandfather's wisdom to the max state
Applying herself as her next step calculates
Even though I bite my tongue when she gets really mad
Still to me—she sounds real crazy and super bad

The Jaguar 45

The Jaguar 45 player always paid deuce
Like true revolutionary working-class crews
My rhymes rise off cement floors like white copal smoke
As the elixirs and remedy antidotes

The night rider returns with a lyrical dose
And a sexy curandera who's very magical
I take flight like the bald eagle over the world
Dropping wordplay hit songs for little boys and girls

I came with heat for this cold world as a pyro
But light the stage and cool it down like I'm hydro
Leaving them wondering about my emcee skills
Spit raw to keep it real bringing chill vibes and thrills

Drum sample machines make me spit back at the cops
Turning my old poetry into raps like a boss
I don't know why but rhyming is the gig I get
Riding over enemies being so legit

Corrupt judges want us to be silenced and hushed
But streets are booming with a psychedelic rush
The Jaguar 45 came prepare for madness
Using sound samples like a lyrical gambit

Here for battle, ready to blast speakers for mass
To overcome jealousy, clown them with a laugh
Survival of the fittest makes no sense to God
As my flow invokes the red star for rebel thugs

My time in jail taught me it's a marketing scheme
Appealing to scare folks that punishment heals fiends
Kids are sent from schools to the prison industry
That's legal human trafficking if you ask me

I'm the spokesman putting my people in glory
Laughing at news reporters with stupid stories
Wearing my thinking cap to make moves for the fans
'In the game for the long-haul slamming, Uncle Sam

Rap City Love Lines

When I met her, she thought I was the criminal
But she was the one who stole my heart and soul
I came into her life but was young and naive
Label hard targets from north to south, west to east

Working two jobs searching for meaningful purpose
We found revolution guiding us to the shores
I'm realizing our bond was born from struggle
As if trouble made us closer and lovable

She never threw me a curved ball as a love goal
My dream catcher in the rye curing me with soul
Never cared about gold, just moving with the wind
Looking for simple truths everywhere that we been

But the hand is quicker than the eye to fight
The heart is quicker than the mind and that's alright
That means that action is greater than ideas from above
Romance always involves deeds greater than two doves

Economic hardships create social outbreaks
While the poor rumble and rich continue to take
Revolutionaries focus on the movement
A social movement for justice to make amends

Gambling with love like revolutionary vets
This is where I stand after hitting my best bet
She puts on a smile with my rap city love lines
Writing about good loving aging like fine wine

Money is a steppingstone into true freedom
Why do rich folk take people's freedom with venom?
It's a contradiction to say that without pain
To rock a diamond while others suffer to gain

It takes a survivor skill to dominate chance
Many forget to have gratitude to advance
Seeking adventure and the greatest mystery—
There's spirit moving through everything you can see

Wolf Heart

I'm illuminating scenes with a lovely queen
Doing the damn thing cause I'm a Harvard Street King
She reps Mexican campesinos with her soul
Saying, "Do it, Lobo. Do it for the people!"

She's singing, "Our love is real," through the bright corn
  field
We're street revolutionaries with the wild skills
Reading bout' Zapata and Che Guevara-
Vanessa Guillen and Zapatista daughters

Wherever we go we're ready for whatever!
The First Natives blessed me with an eagle feather
Car robot films show no love for lowrider streets
We roam Sierra Juarez with guns and machetes

Doing math with raps because I'm badass like that
And my Spoken Word Wife never trips or gets mad
Oaxaca to L.A.—I go hard and insane
Crossing out swastikas with graffiti spray paint

I rock for the creator and great mystery
These cowards sound like busters trying to curse me
But they can't take my gifts, I won't let it happen
I've returned like Odysseus armed and blasting

These two-faced bigots failed the test with no respect
All the women see sucker emcees getting checked
Paid deuce like graffiti boys with laughing static
Blessing the revolution with instant classics

I'm the homeboy who survived the violent filled night
With a passionate kiss for the star in my life—
The one written off as crazy and left alone,
The one doing it slow 'cause I'm bad to the bone

I'm The Harvard Streeter that kept it one-hundred,
The Southsider who was blessed to be a poet,
Blessed by nations to represent beyond borders
The name's Shoktokgiah with the new tribal order!

Chrome Gun Adelita

She always flips your own words like hot tortillas
Making the earth part of her sassy pandilla
Playing with your concepts to break all the nonsense
Add and subtract your metaphors 'til you make cents

She breaks down the game to cleanse it permanently
Her burgundy glasses make her abundantly
Kicking it to the baseline beat using wordplay
I live with her, and it is gracious when we lay

Playing for keeps though some say she doesn't belong
She rocked every open mic with a soothing song
A freedom shepherd under lightning and thunder
The open mic airbender slaying the hunter

Rich folk movie scripts sell out poor people daily
Supporting class warfare even on the babies
But she dreams a revolt to free them from T.V.
Her images make ghetto smiles bright and easy

Even berserk soldiers sweat their brows like saunas
She's clowning like she's the joker baby's mama'
Revolutionary chrome gun Adelitas
Every shot not be wasted cause it's helping us

She practices freedom movements to get good at it
Changing her outfit to honor the sun goddess
Eating wild edibles from the green wilderness
Walking barefoot over rocks to grow foot callus

She multiplies her earnings by hustling her words
Revolutionizing the movement with a swerve
Telling stories of the golden fleece in the breeze
People pay for that when it's off the memory

She rocks duel chrome pistolas to watch this man's back
Blasting those who want to burn down the village shacks
And her knife throwing skills scare off the evil fiends
Trapping them while their creeping like it ain't no thing

Bombs and Poets

They persecute the street poet to cause her harm
She's dangerous to the system with words like bombs
Surviving the matrix with a sweet freedom song
Inspiring the youth to write that which brings the dawn

I knew that she was vital to social changes
But they wanted her dead under such a strange mess
She became the walking dead until I showed up
Blasting evil doers with streetwise music cuts

Letting them know that we aren't going nowhere
Unless we go first class to where no one has dared
She's enticing like thunderstorms with blue lightning
Her poetry hits our hearts leaving her shining

Her words are aimed at ideas to explode them all
With graffiti sentiments like a city wall
Her poetry and gun battle make common sense
Her words are bombs exploding dangerous concepts

When the dusty scenes are clear she's leading the fields
Our opponents suffer 'cause she's breaking the deal
She gains by challenging the evil status quo
Blasting the troops with truth and the red star symbol

The pen is a social justice weapon that heals
Killing pretentious ideas by keeping it real
I'm launching hot verses like Molotov cocktails
Burning the scene while intoxicating females

War doesn't make profit 'til it destroys something
But protecting the poor make us dream better scenes
I too can bomb the system with booming base sound
While getting paid to have the town folk dance around

Women take the lit stage and spit their grievances
Rhyming precisely for the exploited seamstress
It don't take a college degree to make demands
When you make the crowd roar with a microphone stand

If You Ever Sees Us

I sing of a lady who is loved by the poor
She survived dark night's dreaming of ending the war
She's a daring woman with enticing potions
And rides beside me reciting lyric poems

Boulevards are wet after it rains barrio psalms
And sweet freedom songs offered to the morning dawn
The open mic airbenders bends time and space
Breaking evil hexes with kinetic wordplay

I'm traveling through dimensions like a war vet
Blasting enemies with cannons to make her wet
I never surrender to the adversity
While she chants to Mother Earth for the victory

I'm a gangster writing detective mysteries
While she records and spins iambic melodies
We're the page masters with ink pens and sage bundles—
Reciting on lit stages as a dual couple

We smile now and ride out wild as players of words
We're deuces gone wild and metaphor-rhyme hustlers
We're street science mix with poetic physics labs
We pack kinetic energy in our vocab

Living on the edge makes us dangerous
Living like poets from the Marvel Universe
Where our word is our weapon and survival knife
Our kinetic wordplay blazes foes like a pipe

The time machine is a book and memory lapse
Time is money by prison industrial complex
But we spend, make, and take time multiplying lines
Poems foam up like beer and take you to the times

So, if you ever see us throw up a peace sign
We're willing to kick it and share our story lines
Even though we're viewed as rowdy outlaw poets
Our kinetic words can restore the gravel pits

Space Bound Cowboy

We kiss, she feels a rush, she glows and starts to blush
And our love makes her wonder what's in store for us
We're doves and glorious, defeating the sorceress
'Cause when we play the game, we make the haters bust

Playing for keeps makes us dangerous we shoot back
We make them fold showing them their life in pitch black
She treats me like the king, I treat her like my queen
We're clever wherever, forever rocking dreams

We know how we grown, walking this road with our goals
It's no one's life but our own choosing battle roads
She ain't never had a man and a friend like me
Sure 'nuff, it's exactly what I thought it would be

Warm in the twilight showing her heart on her sleeve
Tongue kissing in the snow near the blue river creek
Bless with sweet luck to hold her like answered wishes
Best of the best moments sealed with candy kisses

When we're space bound, she has a blissful expansion
We travel with a fistful of ammunition
Casanova would eat his heart out on my turf
Cause she's my sweet flirt, a sweet supernova bird

Give us field room on a clear summer night in June
Raising our spirit with a big bad sonic boom
'Cause she becomes a butterfly out the cocoon
And I'm a space bound cowboy when we smoke
    mushrooms

The lights and screams, my cash and dreams, a soft verse
    sung
The universal soldier becomes strong at dawn
I'm thanking her with a powerful song and verse
Every star cheers for us when we lay as lovers

We're shuffling our cards on clear summer night in June
Blessing her starlight heart with speakers going boom
'Cause she becomes a butterfly out the cocoon
And I'm a space bound cowboy when we smoke
    mushrooms

Popo and Itza's Revenge

The race against time itself is a hero's tale
Encountering obstacles made to make us fail
The stars are requesting a grand story be told
About two lovebirds facing adversity cold

Wandering over the great Sierra Juarez, Oaxaca
Psychedelic mushrooms are saying, ya basta
Walking planets with a machete and sombrero
I hold her like a star dust shaman guerrero

Traveling the shamanic paths to outer space
Spray painting her name on walls of the Milky Way
Trapped between bipolar movements and conduits
Like the indigenous Romeo and Juliet

Intergalactic gangster with Gala-Chica
Two lovers returning like Popo and Itza
Playing a game of chance to hold the victory
To show love is the answer to the sweet mystery

Class warfare has made a scandal out of love
Raising discouragement at the sight of two doves
Using race to install boundaries that divide
Using social constructs like walls made of old lies

Thrown inside a threshold to forget the soulmate
It was cold, they use her like a pawn and fish bait
To lure the man she loves and strike against her heart
But he shifted her mind to remember the start

When there is a heartbreak to mend you need water
Water has traits to clear every son and daughter
It took lots of water to cleanse the old misdeed
It took a force of earth to be free and happy

The earth is so loving it made us whole again
Made us return to finding love during war and pain
He took speed and haste and aligned time to fend
And now they deal with Popo and Itza's revenge

La Gala-Chica

La Gala-Chica has the confidence to shoot
Any threats against universal attitudes
She blazes the galaxy with lasers and bombs
Orbiting the solar system playing love songs

She wears war paint on her face embarking to hell
Killing demons and trolls that try to rule the world
Blasting through with an army of hell bound girl scouts
When they see Lucifer it's a total knockout

La Gala-Chica passes through speeding meteors
Rocking love songs from earth feeling soft and freer
She caresses the full moon with a victory
Placing her bet to win over the Great Mystery

When the odds are against her all she does is win
Playing for keeps because she's in it till the end
A supernova with her poetry that's wise
This is tale sung from the westside to eastside

They rather kill off the sacred animals first
Then lead awful environmental disasters
The rude awakening of the evil forces
Are threats to all walks of life in many places

She's a beautiful lady grooving space rhythms
Double checking your frequency for true wisdom
Feeding poor children who are hungry and starving
Breaking wicked hexes with a summer party

Meteors are counted by celestial beings
But she must blast her way to survive deadly scenes
Making riches out of her cold lyrical game
Celebrated by a star race that knows no shame

Gala-Chica is short for Gala-Chicana
She survived to be an empress and space shaman
Contacting me when I'm smoking wild peyote
She's my Spoken Word Wife who loves me so dearly

Her Multiverse

I was asked to take flight over the galaxy
Using psychedelic means to kiss my lady
I understood the galactic empress winked fine
Every time I spat metaphors and cold space rhymes

She announced to me that we were always married
That she sent me to earth to cleanse and be daring
That she sent me to earth to win and play for keeps
To be a legend and a dangerous emcee

But I must remain a resident on the planet
Fighting for social justice being a gambit
She said she's the one engaging my truest dreams
Unwinding my memories throughout the whole scene

My Spoken Word Wife came to me in a night's dream
She came from another dimension clearing scenes
Telling me to wordplay and play for keeps all day
We're separated by reality and blue haze

Says she's always been my lovely Spoken Word Wife
She's a galactic empress that purifies life
She exists in a different light reality
She channels through women that are so sweet to me

In a parallel universe reality
She sends me messages telepathically
Igniting her sweet face in the night sky for me
Her lips are made with stars and clouds to be unique

She can take over a woman and speak through her
Sending messages, surprising with experience words
Giving me cues to believe in the feminine
Serving and protecting, defending earth's children

She smiles through the stars and speaks her poetic verse
All these women formed the Spoken Word Wife's
    multiverse
I never ride alone, I'm always blessed with love
To look up at night seeing her sparkling above

Juicy Kid

I'm celebrating with my Spoken Word Wife
Rocking the mic to bring in the cash tonight
It's that Juicy Kid from The Harvard Street Gang
From the City of Angels to make it bang

I'm that Juicy Kid from the block of hard knocks
Cause I dropped black magic witches with non-stop
Hip hop flow and my emcee skills to beat them
A sweet *curandera* kept my heart beating

And many women blessed me when I was young
But this beautiful lady came singing songs
Gracious melodies for the waters of life
That's how I knew she was my Spoken Word Wife

Riding audio waves like a surfing addict
Making her wet when she wears sexy outfits
She glows like embers when I make her all mine
Throwing her love signs for being on my mind

She heats up like vapors and comes down like rain
Forms a stream for my dreams to live with the fame
I stay one hundred for she's my remedy cure
Bumping slow jams in the moonlight being pure

The player of words spits rhymes through space and time
Rising like the sun over her apple lines
I'm here rocking shows with a mighty presence
Bringing cash for kids living in the wastelands

I slam lyrical alchemy to free streets
As Kontombles spit rhymes over hip hop beats
Running through street jungles and boulevard nights
Flowing like a river under the moonlight

I'm the *vato* with iconoclastic flow
Breaking the all-seeing eye with lightning bolts
With freedom fighters destroying the matrix
Freeing boys and girls caged-up by the hatred

Catch me in ritual smoking like a chief
I wore the eagle feather when they named me
Shoktockgia for dropping enemy soldiers
It means wolf in Dakota, fearless warrior

The word doctor breaks curses with a fine nurse
Like illegal laborers in your own turf
Building a movement with underground emcees
Metaphors be with you when you ride the beat

Spitting pyro flows like an oozy machine
Making the party bounce like a trampoline
Playing love songs in my low-low heading home
With my Spoken Word Wife scraping the ozone

I'm celebrating with my Spoken Word Wife

Rocking the mic to bring in the cash tonight
It's that Juicy Kid from The Harvard Street Gang
From the City of Angels to make it bang

Acknowledgements

I'd like to thank the world for inspiring me to write *My Spoken Word Wife*. This book couldn't have happened without the intervention of the voices I am the only one who seems to hear and the hallucinations of women who are asking me to write about them—in a way that makes them larger than life. I would like to thank my mother and family for helping me write this collection. I'd like to thank, my editor and comrade, Dr. Jesú Estrada and co-editor and comrade, Daniel Brooks and long-time mentor, Steve Teixeira for helping me put this work together. A special shout out goes to my homies for believing in me and being a supportive community.

Misael Juarez is a Los Angeles Zapotec who writes to alleviate the intensity of psychosis and schizo-affective disorder, all while achieving a voice for the faceless working-class people, the unjustly caged-up children, the vatos locos coming from the bottom, y las chavas. His works speak to the lonely community of schizophrenics out there. His craft is for those who pay attention to rap lyrics and for lovers of romantic love poetry, barrio ascension, gems of wisdom, and revolutionary and social justice with a touch of wild scenic. *My Spoken Word Wife: Playing for Keeps* highlights all of these themes and aims, and centers on respect for feminine virtues. He's the poetic soldier from every dark corner in the city, a true working-class lyricist.

My Spoken Word Wife: Playing for Keeps is his first collection published with **Barrio Blues Press.**

BOOKS BY BARRIO BLUES PRESS

Nation: A Poetry Book by Penned in the City

Available on Amazon for $5.99 in paperback & $1.99 Kindle/KU.

All proceeds go to the Chicago Freedom School.

Unity, Volume 1: A Magical Realism Anthology

Available on Amazon for $9.99 in paperback & $5.99 Kindle/KU.

All proceeds go to Doctors without Borders.

One Last Favor . . .

You can gift Misael a short review or rating on Amazon, as these reviews support the press and our charity efforts.